INVENTIONS THAT CHANGED THE WORLD

THE CAMERA

BY REBECCA SABELKO

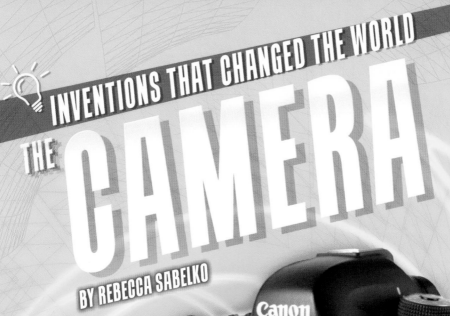

KOHLER ELEMENTARY LIBRARY
KOHLER, WISCONSIN

BLASTOFF!
DISCOVERY

Bellwether Media • Minneapolis, MN

Blastoff! Discovery launches
a new mission: reading to learn.
Filled with facts and features, each
book offers you an exciting new
world to explore!

This edition first published in 2019 by Bellwether Media, Inc.

No part of this publication may be reproduced in whole or in
part without written permission of the publisher.
For information regarding permission, write to Bellwether
Media, Inc., Attention: Permissions Department,
6012 Blue Circle Dr., Minnetonka, MN 55343.

Library of Congress Cataloging-in-Publication Data

Names: Sabelko, Rebecca, author.
Title: The Camera / by Rebecca Sabelko.
Description: Minneapolis, MN : Bellwether Media, Inc., 2019.
   | Series: Blastoff! Discovery. Inventions that Changed the
   World | Includes bibliographical references and index.
   | Audience: Ages 7-13.
Identifiers: LCCN 2018040247 (print)
   | LCCN 2018041685 (ebook) | ISBN
   9781681037011 (ebook) | ISBN 9781626179677
   (hardcover : alk. paper) | ISBN 9781618915108
   (pbk. : alk. paper)
Subjects: LCSH: Photography–History–Juvenile literature. |
   Cameras–Juvenile literature.
Classification: LCC TR149 (ebook) | LCC TR149 .S23 2019
   (print) | DDC 771.3–dc23
LC record available at https://lccn.loc.gov/2018040247

Editor: Betsy Rathburn   Designer: Josh Brink

Printed in the United States of America, North Mankato, MN

TABLE OF CONTENTS

THE BIG APPLE!

Bright neon colors light up each building that towers to the sky. Horns honk from the streets. People rush up and down the crowded sidewalks. Times Square is everything the students imagined it would be!

As they walk down the streets, the students point their smartphones at the sights. One student snaps a photo of an advertisement for the Broadway musical *Wicked*. Another zooms her camera in on a person dressed as Lady Liberty.

Near the Brooklyn Bridge, the students gather to take a selfie. In the background, boats glide across the East River. The friends continue exploring. They snap photos of Central Park, taxicabs, and other sights of New York.

Later, one student captures a shot of Manhattan's skyline. The glass-covered buildings sparkle in the sun. Every way they turn, the students take photos to document their trip. There are so many memories to capture!

PRESERVING MEMORIES

The first camera-like device came from ancient Greece and China. The device was known as *camera obscura*, or the pinhole camera. This "camera" was an entire dark room with a tiny hole in one wall. Light that passed through the hole was projected onto the opposite wall. It showed an upside-down image of the subject outside the hole!

pinhole camera

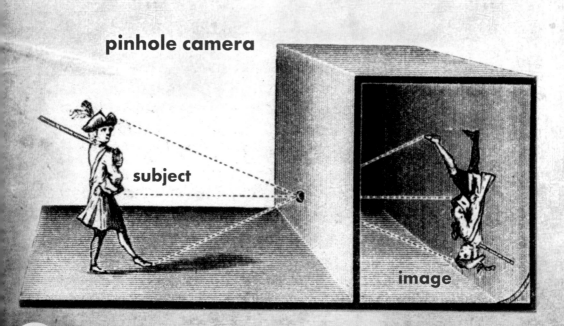

subject

image

pinhole camera

Pinhole cameras were used to observe solar eclipses. The image of the eclipse let people view and study the sun without damaging their eyes. Pinhole cameras did not have film. The only way to keep the images was by tracing them!

In the 1800s, people began to explore ways to keep images. This led to an early film created by Nicéphore Niépce. It was a metal plate coated with **asphalt**. The film was placed inside a small pinhole camera. Images took up to eight hours to **expose**. The images were not permanent unless treated with chemicals.

Nicéphore Niépce

daguerreotype

In 1839, Louis Daguerre made it easier to preserve photos. He created a method that fixed images on paper coated with chemicals. These chemicals needed less exposure time. The resulting images were called daguerreotypes.

The daguerreotype led to a photographic revolution in the late 1800s. A young George Eastman began the Eastman Dry Plate Company in 1881. Throughout the remainder of the century, the company introduced new products that transformed photography.

Eastman's success grew with the introduction of the first transparent film in 1885. His Kodak camera hit the market in 1888, and the idea of the snapshot was born! People could take photos more easily than ever before. Eastman made photography even more available by perfecting transparent roll film in 1889.

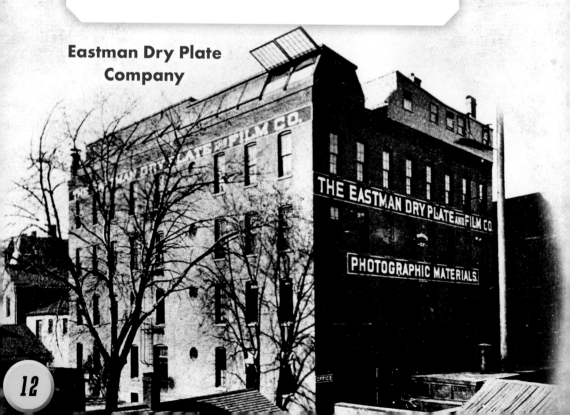

Eastman Dry Plate Company

GEORGE EASTMAN

Born: July 12, 1854, in Waterville, New York

Background: Inventor who worked at an insurance company and a bank before working in photography

Camera Invented: Kodak

Year Invented: 1888

Idea Development: Heavy equipment and a difficult developing process led to Eastman's interest in improving photography. He worked from a previous developing method and found help from local photographers. This led to lighter equipment and easier developing!

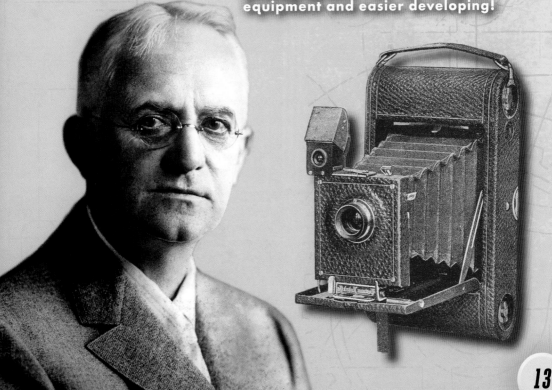

A SNAPSHOT OF THE CAMERA

Eastman continued to create cameras for the public. This led to the creation of the Brownie in 1900. Like the 1888 camera, the Brownie was a simple box camera. But it was much cheaper than any other camera ever made. It cost one dollar!

DID YOU KNOW?

Eastman's favorite letter was K. He wanted the name of his company to begin and end with that letter. With some help, he came up with Kodak!

Part of what made Eastman's Brownie cheap was its simple design. The Brownie was made of cardboard and a simple lens. Its single-speed shutter made it easy to use. The Brownie series of cameras changed the way people recorded their lives through the 1960s.

Ur-Leica

Eastman's Brownie was not the only influential camera of the early 1900s. Oskar Barnack looked to create a smaller camera while studying motion picture film. He developed a **prototype** called Ur-Leica in 1913. This prototype used 35mm film. But the beginning of World War I put a hold on the camera's progress.

Barnack picked up where he left off in 1923. Early tests of his prototype went well. The Leica 1 was introduced in 1924. Today, Barnack's Leica cameras are still popular among photographers around the world!

Leica 1

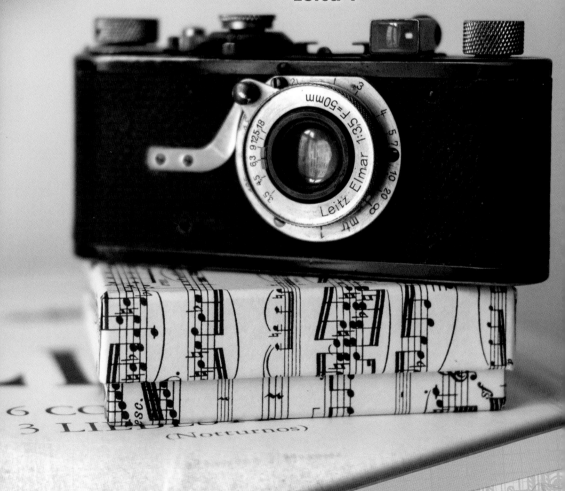

Developments continued into the 1930s. In 1933, the Ihagee company released the Exakta. This was the first **single-lens reflex** (SLR) camera made for regular people. A series of mirrors reflected light into the **viewfinder**. This allowed users to see exactly what their photos would capture!

The Exakta evolved over the coming years to be the first SLR for 35mm film. SLR cameras grew in popularity, and companies worked to expand their features. The Nikon F debuted in 1959 as the first SLR with **interchangeable** parts. It changed professional photography forever!

Exakta

SLR CAMERAS

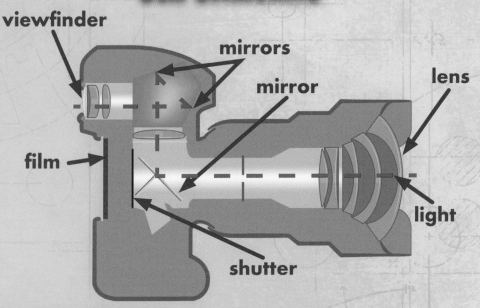

viewfinder

mirrors

mirror

lens

film

light

shutter

When the shutter clicks, light travels through the lens to the exposed film. It bounces off a series of mirrors into the viewfinder.

DID YOU KNOW?

The Polaroid was the first instant-picture camera. The white bar at the bottom of a Polaroid photo held special chemicals. A device in the camera pushed the chemicals through the film.

The late 20th century brought major advancements in technology. One of those was the introduction of the digital camera. Kodak Ektaprint, the first digital camera, arrived in 1975. Sony developed the Mavica in 1981. It stored images on a floppy disk.

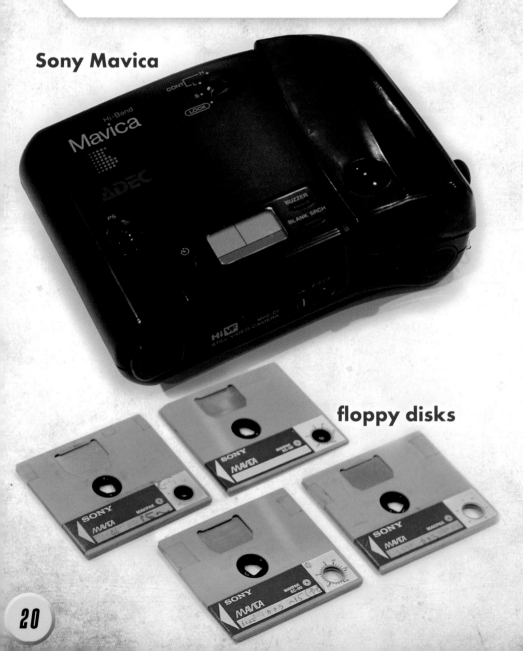

Sony Mavica

floppy disks

Apple QuickTake 100

Digital cameras advanced even further in the 1990s. Cameras like the Kodak DCS 200 and Apple QuickTake 100 could store photos internally. The photos could then be saved to a computer. The Olympus Deltis VC-1100 could send photos to other computers when connected to a computer.

The Nikon D1 became the first digital SLR (DSLR) camera in 1999. About 10 years later, Canon released the EOS 5D Mark II. It had **HD** video!

Camera phones hit the market in 2000 when the J-SH04 was released in Japan. It was the first phone that could send photos electronically! Since then, camera phones have advanced greatly. They include editing tools, videos, and much more!

J-SH04 camera phones

CAMERA PROFILE

NIKON F3

Inventor's Name:	Developed by Nikon with designer Giorgetto Giugiaro
Year of Release:	1980
Uses:	The Nikon F3 was the first camera to take digital photos and store photos on a hard drive. Some Nikon F3 cameras were modified by NASA and used in space!

A WORLD FULL OF PHOTOS

Cameras have played a large role in preserving history. Wars were being photographed as early as the 1850s! Cameras were used during major events throughout the 20th century and beyond. These photographs have created a lasting history!

United States Civil War

Today, digital cameras and smartphones affect the way people take in and share information. People can share photos and videos around the world in a matter of seconds! Having pocket-sized cameras can also help fight crime. Photographic and video proof may be used in many criminal cases.

DIGITAL DAYS

Digital cameras and smartphones will continue to advance to meet the demands of photography. Features like face recognition technology will likely advance. This will help to create more focused photographs.

face recognition

LCD screen

38/38

[248]

FINE

MENU

OK

Mirrorless cameras will likely become more popular. Instead of mirrors, these cameras have an imaging sensor that is exposed to light. They also have an LCD screen that previews images. Many come in small sizes, making them easy to take on the go. Photography will continue to reach people all across the globe!

CAMERA TIMELINE

401-500 BCE

Ancient Chinese writings describe the pinhole camera

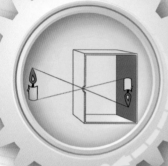

1888

George Eastman introduces the first Kodak camera

1826

Nicéphore Niépce takes the first permanent photograph

1900

The Brownie camera is available to the public for $1.00 and continues to be popular through the 1960s

1975

Steven Sasson invents digital photography and makes the first digital camera

1986

Fuji releases the first disposable camera called QuickSnap

2019-

Future developments

2004

The Epson R-D1 becomes the first mirrorless camera to hit the market

1924

The Leica I is introduced

2001

The Sharp Corporation releases the first camera phone

GLOSSARY

asphalt—a black material used for pavements and as a waterproof cement

box camera—a camera with a simple box shape that has a simple lens and shutter

daguerreotypes—early photographs made on silver-covered copper plates

digital—relating to electronic and computerized technology

expose—to let light hit photographic film while taking a photo; exposure helps an image set.

film—a roll or strip of thin, flexible, transparent material coated with a chemical that is sensitive to light; film is used in taking pictures.

floppy disk—a thin, flexible disk with a magnetic coating that can store information for a computer

HD—high definition; HD images are very clear, digital pictures.

interchangeable—able to put one thing in the place of another thing

lens—a clear, curved piece of material used to bend rays of light to form an image

prototype—an original or first model of something from which other forms are copied or developed

revolution—a sudden, extreme, or complete change

sensor—a device that detects or senses heat, light, sound, or motion and then reacts to it in a particular way

shutter—the part of a camera that opens to allow light in when a picture is taken

single-lens reflex—a camera in which the lens that forms the image on the film also provides the image in the viewfinder

solar eclipses—moments when the sun looks like it is completely or partially covered with a dark circle because the moon is between the sun and the Earth

transparent—able to be seen through

viewfinder—the part of a camera that users look through to see the image that will be produced

TO LEARN MORE

AT THE LIBRARY

Kenney, Karen Latchana. *Who Invented the Movie Camera?: Edison Vs. Friese-Greene.* Minneapolis, Minn.: Lerner Publications, 2018.

Kuskowski, Alex. *Super Simple Camera Projects: Inspiring & Educational Science Activities.* Minneapolis, Minn.: ABDO Publishing, 2016.

Nagelhout, Ryan. *The Problem With Early Cameras.* New York, N.Y.: Gareth Stevens Publishing, 2016.

ON THE WEB

FACTSURFER

Factsurfer.com gives you
a safe, fun way to find
more information.

1. Go to www.factsurfer.com.

2. Enter "camera" into the search box.

3. Click the "Surf" button and select your
   book cover to see a list of related web sites.

INDEX